JAMESTOWN  EDUCATIO

Reading Fluency

Reader

Level
E

Camille L. Z. Blachowicz, Ph.D.

 Glencoe

New York, New York   Columbus, Ohio   Chicago, Illinois   Peoria, Illinois   Woodland Hills, California

JAMESTOWN EDUCATION

 **Glencoe**

The *McGraw·Hill* Companies

Send all inquiries to:
Glencoe/McGraw-Hill
8787 Orion Place
Columbus, OH 43240-4027

ISBN 0-07-830910-7
Printed in the United States of America.
3 4 5 6 7 8 9 10   021   09 08 07 06 05

Contents

The passages in this book are taken from the following sources.

How to Use These Books

The Reading Fluency *Reader* contains 72 reading passages. The accompanying *Reader's Record* contains two copies of each of these passages and includes a place for marking *miscues*.

What Procedure Do I Follow?

1. Read a selection from the *Reader* as your partner marks any miscues you make on the corresponding page in your *Reader's Record*. (A miscue is a reading error. See explanation in How to Use These Books in the *Reader's Record*.) The recorder's job is to listen carefully and make a tick mark above each place in the text where a miscue occurs, and to make a slash mark indicating where you stop reading after "Time!" is called.

2. The recorder says when to start and calls "Time!" after a minute.

3. After the reading, the recorder

   - counts the number of words read, using the number guides at the right-hand side of the passage in the *Reader's Record,* and records the Total Words Read

   - writes the total number of miscues for each line in the far right-hand column labeled Miscues. Totals and records the miscues on the Total Errors line

   - subtracts Total Errors from Total Words Read to find the Correct Words Per Minute (WPM) and records that score on the Correct WPM line

4. Review the *Reader's Record,* noting your miscues. Discuss with your partner the characteristics of good reading you have displayed. Then rate your performance and mark the scale at the bottom of the page.

5. Change roles with your partner and repeat the procedure.

6. You and your partner then begin a second round of reading the same passage. When it is your turn to read, try to improve in pace, expression, and accuracy over the first reading.

7. After completing two readings, record your Correct WPM scores in the back of your *Reader's Record*. Follow the directions on the graph.

from *Watership Down*

by Richard Adams

In the darkness and warmth of the burrow Hazel suddenly woke, struggling and kicking with his back legs. Something was attacking him. There was no smell of ferret or weasel. No instinct told him to run. His head cleared and he realized that he was alone except for Fiver. It was Fiver who was clambering over him, clawing and grabbing like a rabbit trying to climb a wire fence in a panic.

"Fiver! Fiver, wake up, you silly fellow! It's Hazel. You'll hurt me in a moment. Wake up!"

He held him down. Fiver struggled and woke.

"Oh, Hazel! I was dreaming. It was dreadful. You were there. We were sitting on water, going down a great, deep stream, and then I realized we were on a board—like that board [we saw] in the field—all white and covered with black lines. There were other rabbits there—bucks and does. But when I looked down, I saw the board was all made of bones and wire; and I screamed and you said, 'Swim—everybody swim'; and then I was looking for you everywhere and trying to drag you out of a hole in the bank. I found you, but you said, 'The Chief Rabbit must go alone,' and you floated away down a dark tunnel of water."

from "Tuesday of the Other June"

by Norma Fox Mazer

⬦⬦⬦⬦⬦

"Be good, be good, be good, be good, my Junie," my
mother sang as she combed my hair; a song, a story, a
croon, a plea. "It's just you and me, two women alone
in the world, June darling of my heart; we have enough
troubles getting by, we surely don't need a single one
more, so you keep your sweet self out of fighting and all
that bad stuff. People can be little-hearted, but turn the
other cheek, smile at the world, and the world'll surely
smile back."

We stood in front of the mirror as she combed my
hair, combed and brushed and smoothed. Her head came
just above mine; she said when I grew another inch, she'd
stand on a stool to brush my hair. "I'm not giving up this
pleasure!" And she laughed her long honey laugh.

My mother was April, my grandmother had been May,
and I was June. "And someday," said my mother, "you'll
have a daughter of your own. What will you name her?"

"January!" I'd yell when I was little. "February! No,
November!" My mother laughed her honey laugh. She
had little emerald eyes that warmed me like the sun.

from *Homesick*

by Jean Fritz

Our house stood behind a high stone wall which had chips of broken glass sticking up from the top to keep thieves away. I flung open the iron gate and threw myself through the front door.

"I'm home!" I yelled.

Then I remembered that it was Tuesday, the day my mother taught an English class at the Y.M.C.A. where my father was the director.

I stood in the hall, trying to catch my breath, and as always I began to feel small. It was a huge hall with ceilings so high it was as if they would have nothing to do with people. Certainly not with a mere child, not with me—the only child in the house. Once I asked my best friend, Andrea, if the hall made her feel little too. She said no. She was going to be a dancer and she loved space. She did a high kick to show how grand it was to have room.

Andrea Hull was a year older than I was and knew about everything sooner. She told me about commas, for instance, long before I took punctuation seriously. How could I write letters without commas? she asked. She made me so ashamed that for months I hung little wagging comma-tails all over the letters to my grandmother.

Dedicated to a Purpose

Juliette Gordon Low was born in Savannah, Georgia, in 1860. Her uncle called her a "daisy," and the nickname suited her. She was known as "Daisy" throughout her life.

As a young woman, Daisy married a wealthy Englishman. The couple moved to England, and Daisy settled into many years of a life of leisure.

Daisy was forty-five years old when her husband died. She was sad, but she also found herself thinking about life. What had she accomplished?

After several restless years, Daisy met Sir Robert Baden-Powell. He told her about a group he had formed called the Boy Scouts. The purpose of the group was to train boys to live healthy, moral lives. They learned outdoor skills and how to be good citizens.

Sir Robert told Daisy that girls were also interested in scouting. In fact, many had tried to join Boy Scouts. He invited her to help with organizing the girls. His sister had already begun the work. The group was called Girl Guides.

Daisy jumped into the work. She found that she loved it. As she gained experience, her thoughts turned to home.

She would start the first Girl Guides troop in America, right in Savannah.

In time America's Girl Guides would be known as the Girl Scouts.

from *Benjamin Franklin:*
Printer, Inventor, Statesman

by David A. Adler

⟨∝∞∝⟩

In June 1752, he conducted his famous kite and lightning experiment. . . . From the top of the kite, he attached a wire to act as a lightning catcher. To the string he attached a silk ribbon and a key. His son William flew the kite in the midst of a storm. Lightning hit the wire. Benjamin Franklin touched the key and felt a spark. He had proved that lightning is electricity.

Next Franklin made use of his discovery. He invented the lightning rod. In most houses the rods, when struck, carried electricity into the ground where it would do no harm. But this was not true in Benjamin Franklin's house. In his house, the rod led to two bells with a . . . ball between them. When lightning hit the rod, sparks flew, making the bells ring.

Franklin experimented with ants, too. He hung a clay pot filled with molasses from a string nailed to the ceiling. In the pot was a single ant. Franklin waited and watched. When the ant had eaten the molasses, it left the pot, climbed the string to the ceiling, and then climbed down the wall. Shortly after that a parade of ants found their way to the molasses, because, Franklin was sure, the first ant somehow told them where it was. Ants, he concluded, had a way of communicating with each other.

from *The Wind in the Willows*
by Kenneth Grahame

After they had chatted for a time about things in general, the Badger said, "Now, then! Tell us the news from your part of the world. How's old Toad going on?"

"O, from bad to worse," said the Rat gravely; while the Mole, basking in the firelight, his heels higher than his head, tried to look properly mournful. "Another smashup only last week, and a bad one. You see, he will insist on driving himself, and he's hopelessly incapable. If he'd only employ a steady, well-trained animal, pay him good wages, and leave things to him, he'd get on all right. But no; he's convinced he's a heaven-born driver, and nobody can teach him anything. All the rest follows."

"How many has he had?" asked the Badger.

"Smashes, or machines?" asked the Rat. "O, well, after all, it's the same thing—with Toad. This is the seventh. As for the others—you know that coach house of his? Well, it's piled up—piled up to the roof—with fragments of cars none of them bigger than your hat! That accounts for the other six—as far as they can be accounted for."

"He's been in the hospital three times," put in the Mole. "And as for the fines he's had to pay, it's simply awful to think of."

7

Fiction

from *The Curse of the Blue Figurine*

by John Bellairs

"I . . . I . . ." Johnny began, but he couldn't get the words out. Rooted to the spot with fear, he watched as Eddie began walking slowly toward him. And then something strange and totally unexpected happened. Johnny felt a sharp pain in his ring finger, and it seemed to him that the yellow stone flashed. And then a strong wind began to blow. It sprang up out of nowhere and blew past Johnny. The bushes that grew in the courtyard flailed madly to and fro. Bits of paper sailed up into the air, and a cloud of yellowish dust flew at Eddie. Coughing and sputtering, Eddie staggered backward. The wind blew harder and threw him, stumbling and reeling, against the brick wall. Bottles flew this way and that, and when Eddie stuck out a hand to steady himself, it came down on a piece of broken glass.

Eddie howled and jerked his hand toward his mouth. He sucked at the bleeding cut. Then silence fell. The wind died as suddenly as it had sprung up, and the yellow dust settled. Eddie looked at Johnny, and Johnny looked at Eddie. And which of them was more frightened it would have been hard to say.

Pronunciation Guide

flailed: flāld

8
Nonfiction

from *The Exxon Valdez: Tragic Oil Spill*

by Victoria Sherrow

⌇⌇⌇

The roots of the *Exxon Valdez* disaster date back to 1968. That year, large deposits of oil were found on Alaska's North Slope. Oil . . . is a valued source of energy. It is often called black gold. The United States uses more oil than any other country in the world.

Many people were glad to hear about new sources of oil in the United States. Few nations have vast oil deposits. Most oil-rich countries are located in the Middle East. Some of those countries, such as Iran, have clashed with the United States. Their control over oil had enabled them to set high prices. Alaskan oil would make the United States less dependent on foreign imports.

Oil would also bring new jobs to Alaska. Thousands of people would be needed to set up wells and drill for oil. Others would work to build a pipeline for moving the oil to other parts of the state. The oil companies would need many employees for years to come.

The state of Alaska would earn hundreds of millions of dollars by selling drilling rights to oil companies. These businesses would also pay high taxes to the state.

Plans were made to start drilling in Prudhoe Bay, on the Arctic Coast.

Pronunciation Guide

Exxon Valdez: ek' son   väl dēz'   Prudhoe: prə' dō

9

Fiction

from *Dragonwings*

by Laurence Yep

I watched helplessly as [our flying machine] Dragonwings started to turn, but the right side of its wings brushed the hillside. The wooden frame of the right wings snapped in a dozen places. Broken wooden poles ripped through the canvas as it flapped upward. The left wings rose leisurely until they were almost straight up, and then Dragonwings leaned forward and burrowed nose first into the hillside. The body of Dragonwings swung back and forth drunkenly and then hung at an odd angle.

I raced toward Dragonwings, feeling as if I had been betrayed. Somehow, after we had lavished so much time and effort and money on it, it should never have let one of its bolts snap and destroy itself and maybe kill Father. Father had been thrown clear of Dragonwings and lay on his back. I took his wrist. He still had a pulse.

Puffing, Uncle joined me. It was surprising that he could run at all, let alone outdistance the others. It must have been as Uncle always said: There was a lot of life still left in his old beat-up body. Uncle dropped to his knees beside me and, with delicate hands, felt Father's bones. The others gathered around, catching their breaths. Finally Uncle straightened and looked around, relieved.

Pronunciation Guide

lavished: lav' ishd

from *Charlotte Forten: Free Black Teacher*

by Esther M. Douty

Charlotte liked the Remond home on Dean Street. It was not as fine and spacious as the Forten home in Philadelphia, but it was well furnished and large enough for Charlotte to have her own room, which overlooked an old-fashioned flower garden.

Beyond the garden Charlotte could see other quiet, tree-shaded streets. Which one of these, she wondered, led to the Higginson School for Girls? And which led to the Remond Hair Works where the family earned its living by weaving wigs and hair pieces for men and women?

In the morning her father walked with her to school. As they picked their way over the uneven old brick sidewalks, he said, "You know, Charlotte, there are 188 girls at the school. You will be the only one who isn't white."

"Yes, father, I know." Charlotte's gentle voice was a bit sharp. Father had told her this before. So had her aunts. And her grandmother. And the Purvises. And the Anti-Slavery Society ladies. She was tired of hearing it. Then a glance at her father's face made her say, as she always did, "Don't worry. I'll study hard. I'll prove to the others that a dark skin does not mean a second-rate mind."

Pronunciation Guide

spacious: spā′ shəs

from *The Moon of the Moles*

by Jean Craighead George

[The mole] had excavated four miles of runways, but he had never made a door or an exit to the sky. The top of the earth was not for him. It was not cozy enough. He needed walls and tight low ceilings, where he could live a snuggly secret life.

Upon settling down under the wheat field he had first dug a round chamber beneath rock in the creek bank. This he filled with rootlets and bits of root bark to make his bed. Then he excavated the runways from this central station until he had five major tunnels. One, the Wheat Root Run, tunneled under the field. Another followed the creek to the east. A third went west beneath the bridge and the road that led to the cattle shed and farmhouse. Another branched off and led up the roadside, while the fifth wandered among the cottonwood roots in the creek bottom.

The mole ran all of these without seeing. Moles have lived in the ground for so long that their eyes have become functionless. Skin grows over them. The eyes are mere specks on either side of the head, too small to register anything but lightness and darkness. Some moles live all their one to three years of life without ever knowing light.

Pronunciation Guide

excavated: eks′ kə vā′ td

12

Nonfiction

from ***Within Reach:***
My Everest Story

by Mark Pfetzer and Jack Galvin

───────────────◦◦◦───────────────

[There is] nothing worse than two guys yanking on a rope from two directions when you have to [use an ascender to go] up a steep section. This is steep. And scary. We're on a rock face that's about vertical. And on the rock face, there is a ledge that you have to scoot across sideways, then get up on top of the ledge and over the rock face.

What gets scary is you are on a face that is 5,000 feet straight down. I clip onto the rope and start to work my way across the ledge. I have to twist one leg against the rock face, squish around for a handhold, then swing my body out, leaning into the side of the rock so I can get my two feet balanced on little nubs of rock. I can only look down at my feet and, consequently, down to the reddish-brown valley far below. Rock climbers do this stuff all the time. I've done it myself, but there are some big differences. Like the twenty-five pound backpack I'm carrying, which gets stuck in the gap in the rock face. Like the incredible feeling of height on the razor-thin ledge on this vertical ridge.

Pronunciation Guide

ascender: ə sen′ dər

The Father of Sherlock Holmes

Who hasn't heard of Sherlock Holmes? At the mention of Holmes's name, one pictures a tall, lean, sharp-faced detective. He sweeps out of his lodgings at 221B Baker Street. In cape and deerstalker cap, he calls back, "Come, Watson! The game is afoot!"

Sherlock Holmes was not a real person. He came to life from the imagination of Arthur Conan Doyle. In the late 1880s, Conan Doyle was a young doctor. He began writing stories to earn extra money.

A Study in Scarlet introduced Holmes and his friend, Dr. John Watson, to the public. The book was published in 1887. *The Sign of Four* followed. In 1891, Conan Doyle began a series of stories for *Strand* magazine. The series was called *The Adventures of Sherlock Holmes.*

Conan Doyle once said that he modeled Holmes after a teacher he'd had, Dr. Joseph Bell. Bell was quick and an excellent logician. Once Bell glanced at a corpse on the anatomy table. From this glance, he deduced that the person had been a left-handed shoemaker.

"It is all very well to say that a man is clever," Conan Doyle once wrote. "But the reader wants to see examples of it—such examples as Bell gave us every day."

Coretta Scott King:
The Dream Lives On

Coretta Scott King was married to one of the greatest civil rights leaders of all time, Dr. Martin Luther King, Jr. She helped her husband in many ways and was often at his side. After King's death, she became a leader in her own right.

Coretta Scott was born in Alabama in 1927. Her father ran a small store and, to help make ends meet, also hauled lumber as a second job. Her mother worked too, driving a school bus. Young Coretta pitched in, picking cotton to earn money.

In some ways, life was hard for Coretta. She had to walk five miles each day to school. But the walk wasn't as hard as watching the school bus pass her by. The bus was for white children only. Such unfair treatment stung. Someday, she vowed, people would treat her as an equal.

Coretta's high school teachers were the first college graduates that she had known. She saw that people with education had more choices in life and were treated with respect. She decided that going to college would improve her life.

Coretta Scott studied hard to make her dream come true. She finished first in her high school class. Then she went on to Antioch College, where she studied to be a teacher.

Pronunciation Guide

Antioch: an′ tē ok′

from *The Pistachio Prescription*

by Paula Danziger

I just don't fit in with the rest of my family. I'm sure I'm adopted, that I'm a Martian they found in the backyard and took in for the tax deduction. No one else in the family looks like me. Two have curly red hair and green eyes, my mother and Andrew. My father and Stephie have blond hair and blue eyes. I've got brown hair and brown eyes. The only one I resemble is Mutant, my brother's pet gerbil.

Everyone else has normal names—Andrew, Anne, Andrew, Jr., and Stephanie. I got named Cassandra. Just my luck that my mother was taking a course in Greek mythology right before I was born. (So they say, but I bet they're just trying to make me think I'm not adopted.) Every year, some teacher tells me how it was Cassandra's curse to speak the truth and be thought insane. If that happens one more time, I'm going to scream. Sometimes I'm afraid I'll end up like that other Cassandra. Maybe they make straitjackets in prewashed denim. . . .

My parents are difficult. That's what they're always saying about me, but they're impossible. Sometimes they are wonderful, sometimes terrible, and I never know which one it's going to be.

Pronunciation Guide

Mutant: my͞oot' nt   straitjackets: strāt' jak' itz

16

Nonfiction

from *Dark Harvest:*
Migrant Farmworkers in America
by Brent Ashabranner

"It was a hard life, but there were good things about it, too. The family was always together, and we usually traveled with five or six other families, so we were with people we knew. We were all poor, so we were all the same. And we could still have good times together.

"Sometimes on a Saturday, we would not work or stop work early. We would go to town crowded in the back of a truck, maybe twenty or thirty young men and women, to buy food and clothes. . . . If there was money, my father would give us each a dollar. We would eat ice cream and go to a Western movie.

"Sometimes someone asks me if I was envious of people I saw in towns who had good homes and good clothes and big new cars. No, I wasn't. They belonged to another world, a world I didn't know anything about. But there was one thing from that world that I did want. I loved music and I always wanted a record player. I used to look at them in the stores, but, of course, I was never able to buy one."

Pronunciation Guide

envious: en′ vē əs

from *I Have Lived a Thousand Years*

by Livia Bitton-Jackson

Our homeroom teacher had just made the shocking announcement: "Class, the Royal Hungarian Ministry of Education . . . to safeguard our best interests . . . has terminated instruction in all the nation's schools. Effective immediately." Her voice broke. She swallowed hard. "Our school is closed, as of now."

It is Saturday, March 25th, 1944. Six days have passed since the Germans invaded Budapest. What about graduation, only three months away? What about our report cards?

But [our teacher] leaves the classroom before we have a chance to ask questions. She leaves without a word of reference to the German occupation. Without indication of what is to happen next.

We sit in stunned silence, staring at each other. And then slowly, ever so slowly, my classmates stand up one by one and file out of the classroom.

I, too, rise to my feet and look around. The worn, wood benches bolted to the dark, oil-stained floor. The whitewashed walls with their threadbare maps and faded pictures. It is all so familiar, so reassuring. . . .

For nearly four years I have struggled, sweated, and sometimes triumphed within these walls. In front of this blackboard. For nearly four years I have breathed the smell of the oiled floor mingled with chalk dust, apprehension, and excitement.

Will I ever again sit behind this narrow desk?

18

Fiction

from *The Black Stallion*
by Walter Farley

Huge waves swept from one end of the *Drake* to the other. Hysterical passengers crowded into the corridor. Alec was genuinely scared now; never had he seen a storm like this!

For what seemed hours, the *Drake* plowed through wave after wave, trembling, careening on its side, yet somehow managing to stay afloat. The long streaks of lightning never diminished; zigzagging through the sky, their sharp cracks resounded on the water.

From the passageway, Alec saw one of the crew make his way along the deck in his direction, desperately fighting to hold on to the rail. The *Drake* rolled sideways and a huge wave swept over the boat. When it had passed, the sailor was gone. The boy closed his eyes and prayed.

The storm began to subside a little and Alec felt new hope. Then suddenly a bolt of fire seemed to fall from the heavens above them. A sharp crack and the boat shook. Alec was thrown flat on his face, stunned. Slowly he regained consciousness. He was lying on his stomach; his face felt hot and sticky. He raised his hand, and withdrew it covered with blood. Then he became conscious of feet stepping on him. The passengers, yelling and screaming, were climbing, crawling over him! The *Drake* was still— its engines dead.

Pronunciation Guide

hysterical: hi ster′ i kəl   careening: kə rēn′ ing

from "Stop the Sun"

by Gary Paulsen

Terry Erickson was a tall boy, 13, starting to fill out with muscle but still a little awkward. He was on the edge of being a good athlete, which meant a lot to him. He felt it coming too slowly, though, and that bothered him.

But what bothered him even more was when his father's eyes went away.

Usually it happened when it didn't cause any particular trouble. Sometimes during a meal his father's fork would stop halfway to his mouth, just stop, and there would be a long pause while the eyes went away, far away.

After several minutes his mother would reach over and take the fork and put it gently down on his plate, and they would go back to eating—or try to go back to eating—normally.

They knew what caused it. When it first started, Terry had asked his mother in private what it was, what was causing the strange behavior.

"It's from the war," his mother had said. "The doctors at the veterans' hospital call it Vietnam syndrome."

"Will it go away?"

"They don't know. Sometimes it goes away. Sometimes it doesn't. They are trying to help him."

"But what happened? What actually caused it?"

"I told you. Vietnam."

Pronunciation Guide

syndrome: sin′ drōm

Tragedy and Rescue at Sea

Just after midnight on July 30, 1945, two Japanese torpedoes slammed into the USS *Indianapolis*. There were 1,196 men on board the *Indianapolis* at the time. The explosions caught most of them sleeping.

From the time it was hit, the ship took only 12 minutes to sink. About 400 men went down with her. The rest of the crew, many badly wounded, either slipped off the tilting deck or jumped into the sea.

While some were killed by sharks, others died from their wounds. And more died after going insane from the endless fear combined with a lack of sleep and no fresh water.

The sailors spent four days and five nights drifting in the water. By then, without water to drink, they were all near death. But their will to live paid off. By chance, a U.S. Navy patrol plane spotted the survivors. The pilot wiggled the plane's wings to let them know he had seen them in the vast sea below. He radioed their location and the next morning—at last—rescue ships arrived. Three hundred sixteen men survived the ordeal. Eight hundred eighty others didn't. It was the worst wartime loss of life at sea in U.S. Navy history.

21

Fiction

from *So Big*

by **Edna Ferber**

It was in the third year of Selina's marriage that she first went into the fields to work. Pervus had protested miserably, though the vegetables were spoiling in the ground.

"Let them rot," he said. "Better the stuff rots in the ground. DeJong women folks . . . never worked in the fields. Not even in Holland. Not my mother or my grandmother. It isn't for women."

Selina . . . felt steel-strong and even hopeful again, sure signs of physical well-being. Long before now she had realized that this time must inevitably come. So she answered briskly, "Nonsense, Pervus. Working in the field's no harder than washing or ironing or scrubbing or standing over a hot stove in August. Women's work! Housework's the hardest work in the world. That's why men won't do it."

She would often take the boy Dirk with her into the fields, placing him on a heap of empty sacks in the shade. He invariably crawled off this lowly throne to dig and burrow in the warm black dirt. He even made as though to help his mother, pulling at the rooted things with futile fingers, and sitting back with a bump when a shallow root did unexpectedly yield to his tugging.

"Look! He's a farmer already," Pervus would say.

But within Selina something would cry, "No! No!"

Pronunciation Guide

DeJong: dē yong'   futile: fyo͞ot' il

22

Fiction

from *Taking Sides*

by Gary Soto

The basketball echoed in the Columbus Junior High School gym, where banners of the team's championship years—1980, 1987, and 1989—hung from the rafters.

"Bukowski, breathe on him. Maneuver left—now cut, Grady! Press!"

Shoes squeaked as the players hustled up and down the court. The fluorescent lights hummed overhead, and the heater blew warm, dusty air. A few students sat cross-legged on the floor, books piled in their laps, watching. In a far corner, three cheerleaders bounced from foot to foot, chanting "Hey! Hey! Whatta you say!" It was practice hour for them, too.

Lincoln blew past the center, Grady, and, leaping to his left, slammed the ball through the hoop. He came down hard, jamming his already-hurt toe. He stopped for a moment, grimacing, then hobbled after the other players, a spark of pain flashing in his foot.

"Come on!" Coach hissed, as he ran his hands through his hair.

He blew a whistle that hung on a chain around his wrist and whacked his clipboard against his thigh. The players came to a stop. The sound of their breathing filled the gym as they stood with hands on their hips. One player knelt down on one knee, but he rose when Coach gave him an angry look. The cheerleaders, oblivious to the game, raised their arms and screamed.

Pronunciation Guide

grimacing: grim′ əs ing   oblivious: ə bliv′ ē əs

22

from "Snowfall in Childhood"
by Ben Hecht

At three o'clock we rushed into the storm. Our screams died as we reached the school entrance. What we saw silenced us. Under the dark sky the street lay piled in an unbroken bank of snow. And above it the snowfall still hung in a thick and moving cloud. Nothing was visible but snow. Everything else had disappeared. Even the sky was gone.

I saw the teachers come out and look around them, frowning. The children of the lower grades stood chattering and frightened near the teachers. I waited until the teacher with the two black braids saw me, and then, paying no attention to her warning, spoken in a gentle voice, I plunged into the storm. I felt brave but slightly regretful that Miss Wheeler could no longer see me as I pushed into the head-high piles of snow and vanished fearlessly into the storm. But I was certain that she was still thinking of me and worrying about my safety. This thought added excitement to the snowstorm.

After an hour I found myself alone. My legs were tired with jumping and my face burned. It had grown darker and the friendliness seemed to have gone out of the storm. The wind bit with a sharper edge and I turned toward my home.

from *The Autobiography of Miss Jane Pittman*

by Ernest J. Gaines

⬦⬦⬦

We ate and started walking, going North all the time. I watched the ground getting blacker and more damp. With the sun straight up we came to the bayou that . . . we had been headed toward for so long. Now, I had to carry Ned and the bundle, the bundle on my head, Ned on my hip. The water came up to my knees most the time, and sometimes it even got high as my waist. How I made it over only the Lord knows. But I made it and found a good place to sit down and rest. By the time I had rested, my dress had dried out, and we started walking again. We came in another thicket where they had had plenty fighting. You could see how cannon balls had knocked limbs and bark off the trees. It had a mound of dirt there about half the size of my gallery where they had buried many soldiers. They had put a cross at one end of the grave with a cap stuck on top of the cross. The weather had changed the color of the cap so much you couldn't tell if it [belonged] to a Yankee or Secesh. We sat there and rested awhile and I told Ned not to be scared.

Pronunciation Guide

bayou: bī′ o͞o   Secesh: sə sesh′

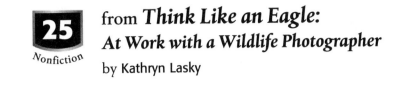

from *Think Like an Eagle: At Work with a Wildlife Photographer*

by Kathryn Lasky

25

Nonfiction

⸻ ⊶⊷ ⸻

He follows a silver thread of moonlight through the forest. The tangled shadows of bare-branched trees spread across the snowy ground. His breath comes in great clouds, and the only sound is the soft crunch of his boots in the snow. Over the past thirty years or more, he has often walked through these woods. He knows the way even on a moonless night. He is never lost. On his back he carries a pack, and in each hand he holds a cylindrical case. In the backpack and the cases are lenses and cameras and films. These are his tools. Jack Swedberg is a wildlife photographer.

Now Jack crosses a stream that feeds into the reservoir. The water slides like a black satin ribbon under snow bridges and curls around billowing white banks. He is coming near the edge of the forest, where the reservoir begins. Frozen solid and glistening white, the water reflects the moon's light like a huge shield of battered silver.

Jack is wrapped in the silence of the forest when suddenly from somewhere behind him, deep in the heart of the woods, comes the flat *hooo hoooo* of the great horned owl. *Hooo hoooo.* The call thrums through the forest.

Pronunciation Guide

cylindrical: si lin′ dri kəl   reservoir: rez′ ər vwär

from *Laura:*
The Life of Laura Ingalls Wilder
by Donald Zochert

———————⊙⊙⊙———————

One day, when Plum Creek roared at its loudest, danger came to the little house like an uninvited guest. Laura [Ingalls Wilder] told about it many years later in her memoir. Ma had suddenly become desperately sick, and Pa's thin face was a mask of worry. He couldn't leave her, because she was in pain, and he could do nothing to help her. She needed a doctor. He turned to Laura and told her to run up to Mr. Nelson's house. Mr. Nelson would ride to town and telegraph for the doctor to come, Pa said. But he had forgotten one thing: the brown, foamy fingers of Plum Creek sweeping dangerously against the footbridge Laura would have to cross.

Laura was frightened, but she knew she had to go. Pa had said so. She slipped from the house and raced down the path toward the creek. And there she stopped. The creek roared around the curving bank and battered the fragile bridge. Some of the water, yellow and shiny, slid smoothly over the top of the log stepping boards. At both ends of the bridge, flood-waters swirled and circled in treacherous pools.

The bridge was an island! Laura's eyes grew wider; she looked at it for a moment and stepped carefully into the nearest pool. It was the only way to reach the bridge.

Pronunciation Guide

memoir: mem′ wär   fragile: fraj′ əl
treacherous: trech′ ər əs

Runaway Bus

The day started quietly enough for 10-year-old Larry Champagne III of St. Louis, Missouri. As usual, he boarded the school bus at about 7:25 A.M. The ride to school was a long one, so Larry settled back in his seat.

Suddenly, Larry and the other children felt the bus swerve. Looking up, they saw the driver collapse, falling completely out of her seat and landing on the bus's stairwell. The children knew they were in trouble.

The bus, now totally out of control, careened across three lanes of traffic and banged against the guardrails on the side of the highway. Outside, drivers who saw the runaway bus honked their horns and swerved out of the way, but there was nothing they could do to save the children trapped inside.

Then, all of a sudden, Larry jumped out of his seat. He ran down the aisle and slid into the driver's seat. Larry knew what to do. He grabbed the steering wheel with his hands while his foot felt around for the brake. When he located it, he stomped down on it hard.

Moments later Larry managed to bring the bus to a complete halt. The children could barely believe it; they were all still alive! Larry Champagne's courage and quick thinking had brought them through the morning's events unscathed.

Pronunciation Guide

Champagne: sham pān'
careened: kə rēnd'

unscathed: un skā*th*d'

from *The Contender*

by Robert Lipsyte

"Stick and run, stick and run," whispered Donatelli in his ear, but Alfred was listening to the ring announcer, "In white trunks, from the Bronx, weighing one hundred thirty-six pounds, Joe Rivera. In black trunks, from Harlem, New York, weighing one hundred thirty-four and three-quarters pounds, Alfred Brooks."

The soft, warm terry cloth slipped off his shoulders and Bud's dry stick-fingers were stabbing into his back muscles. "Stick and run, don't slug with him, stick and run, jab and move." Henry shoved the mouthpiece in.

Hands pushed him into the center of the ring and the referee was saying, ". . . three rounds of two minutes each . . . you know the amateur rules . . . break clean . . . shake, boys, and come out fighting."

The ice ball exploded, spraying his entire body with freezing, paralyzing streams of water, weighing down his arms, deadening his legs, squeezing his heart.

"Stick and run, don't . . ."

The bell rang. He moved numbly forward on stiff legs. Rivera's beady black eyes stared at him over a bent nose.

"Move, Alfred, for . . ."

He walked right into it, a ton of concrete that slammed into his mouth. His arms flew up, and he staggered backwards on his heels. The ropes burned into his back.

Pronunciation Guide

paralyzing: par′ ə līz′ ing

The World's Greatest Athlete?

Many people are good in one athletic event. A few excel in two. But very few can compete in a sport requiring skill in seven different events. Jackie Joyner-Kersee is someone who could. Some have called her the world's greatest athlete.

Even as a child, Jackie Joyner wanted to do well in many sports. In high school she competed in volleyball, basketball, and track. Basketball was her favorite sport then. She attended college on a four-year basketball scholarship. She became a basketball All-American.

After marrying her coach, Bob Kersee, Jackie began focusing on track. One of her best events was always the long jump. Over the years Joyner-Kersee has won many long jump medals. These include an Olympic gold medal and several world championships.

What about the sport with seven different events? It is called the heptathlon. Besides long jump, it includes events like hurdles, high jump, and shot put. Joyner-Kersee competed in this sport in four different Olympics. She won two gold medals and one silver.

Joyner-Kersee has succeeded for two reasons. Her great athletic ability is one thing. But she also possesses great mental toughness. That toughness helped her triumph in spite of her serious asthma and allergies.

Pronunciation Guide

heptathlon: hep tath' lon

The End of John Dillinger

According to police, master criminal John Dillinger was betrayed by one of his girlfriends. Anna Sage came to the Chicago police. She offered to take them to Dillinger. In return, they agreed to help her get out of some legal troubles.

Police records show that on July 22, 1934, Sage went to a movie with Dillinger. She wore a red dress so police agents could spot her in the crowd. When she walked out of the theater with Dillinger, six agents moved in. Three of them fired at Dillinger, who dropped to the ground, dead.

But another version of the story says that it was not John Dillinger who died outside a Chicago theater that day. According to this story, Anna Sage tricked police. Some people claim her unfortunate companion was really a small-time crook named Jimmy Lawrence.

There are a few facts to support this theory. Doctors said they found no scars on the dead man. But Dillinger's body should have shown a couple of old bullet wounds. Also, doctors said the dead man's eyes were brown. Dillinger's were blue.

It may be that the doctors were sloppy when they examined Dillinger's body. Or it may be that police shot the wrong man. We'll never know for sure.

from *Lost Star:*
The Story of Amelia Earhart

by Patricia Lauber

The tropical sun blazed in a blue sky, and the plane glittered as it taxied toward one end of the airfield. Its pilot was Amelia Earhart, whose daring flights had made her famous. With her navigator Fred Noonan, she was attempting what had never been done before: a flight around the world at the equator. So far they had flown 22,000 miles in less than a month. Now they were starting the final legs of the trip.

The plane reached the end of the runway, and Amelia swung it around. Home was 7,000 miles away, on the far side of the Pacific Ocean, and she yearned to be there. But one thing at a time. At this moment her job was to get the plane safely off the ground. The runway stretching ahead was a strip carved out of the jungle. About 3,000 feet long, it ended at a cliff that dropped away into the ocean.

Amelia pushed both throttles forward. The plane moved slowly, heavy with fuel for the long ocean flight that lay ahead. At last it began to gather speed. It went faster and faster, hurtling toward the cliff. Almost at the very edge she felt it leave the ground.

Pronunciation Guide

Amelia Earhart: ə mēl′ yə   är′ härt

32

Fiction

from "The Kid Nobody Could Handle"

by Kurt Vonnegut Jr.

⌀⌀⌀

Helmholtz's first class of the morning was C Band, where beginners thumped and wheezed and tooted as best they could, and looked down the long, long, long road through B Band to A Band, the Lincoln High School Ten Square Band, the finest band in the world.

Helmholtz stepped onto the podium and raised his baton. "You are better than you think," he said. "A-one, a-two, a-three." Down came the baton.

C Band set out in its quest for beauty—set out like a rusty switch engine, with valves stuck, pipes clogged, unions leaking, bearings dry.

Helmholtz was still smiling at the end of the hour, because he'd heard in his mind the music as it was going to be someday. His throat was raw, for he had been singing with the band for the whole hour. He stepped into the hall for a drink from the fountain.

As he drank, he heard the jingling of chains. He looked up at Jim Donnini. Rivers of students flowed between classrooms, pausing in friendly eddies, flowing on again. Jim was alone. When he paused, it wasn't to greet anyone, but to polish the toes of his boots on his trousers legs. He had the air of a spy in a melodrama, missing nothing.

Pronunciation Guide

Donnini: dō nē′ nē   eddies: ed′ ēz

from *The Star Fisher*

by Laurence Yep

Fiction

My little brother, Bobby, was thumping his heels rhythmically against the [train] seat. At ten, he was easily bored. During the day, he was like lightning, always having to dart here and there. He would never walk when he could run. And then in the evenings, he would just conk out suddenly. Mama used to wish we could bottle some of his energy and sell it for tonic.

"When are we going to get there?" Bobby asked for the twentieth time.

Bobby had meant his question for me, so he had used English; but Mama spoke to him in Chinese. "Speak in your own language." Though both Mama and Papa wore American clothes, that was about the only thing American about them, since they spoke little English.

"He wanted to know when we would be arriving in town," I translated for Mama, the way I usually did.

However, Mama was staring straight at Bobby. "Let him answer for himself."

Bobby dragged a finger back and forth along the windowsill. "Mama, people stare when we use Chinese."

"Let them stare," Mama said. "I don't want you to forget your Chinese."

"As if I could," Bobby muttered in English.

from *Slam!*

by Walter Dean Myers

Basketball is my thing. I can hoop. Case closed. I'm six four and I got the moves, the eye, and the heart. You can take my game to the bank and wait around for the interest. With me it's not like playing a game, it's like the only time I'm being for real. Bringing the ball down the court makes me feel like a bird that just learned to fly. I see my guys moving down in front of me and everything feels and looks right. Patterns come up and a small buzz comes into my head that starts to build up and I know it won't end until the ball swishes through the net. If somebody starts messing with my game it's like they're getting into my head. But if I've got the ball it's okay, because I can take care of the situation. That's the word and I know it the same way I know my tag, Slam. Yeah, that's it. Slam. But without the ball, without the floorboards under my feet, without the mid-court line that takes me halfway home, you can get to me.

So when Mr. Tate, the principal at my new school, started talking about me laying low for the season until I got my grades together I was like seriously turned out.

35

Fiction

from "Naftali the Storyteller and His Horse, Sus"

by Isaac Bashevis Singer

─────────── ⬿⬿⬿ ───────────

That night Zelig was despondent. When his wagon was empty of passengers, his wallet was empty of money, and there wouldn't be enough for [his wife] to prepare for the Sabbath.

Suddenly Zelig saw lying in the road a sack that appeared to be full of flour or ground sugar. Zelig stopped his horse and got down to take a look. A sack of flour or sugar would come in handy in a household.

Zelig untied the sack, opened it, took a lick, and decided that it was ground sugar. He lifted the sack, which was unusually heavy. Zelig was accustomed to carrying his passengers' baggage and he wondered why a sack of sugar should feel so heavy.

It seems I didn't have enough to eat at the inn, Zelig thought. And when you don't eat enough, you lose your strength.

He loaded the sack into the wagon. It was so heavy that he nearly strained himself.

He sat down on the driver's box and pulled on the reins, but the horse didn't move.

Zelig tugged harder and cried out . . . "Giddap!"

But even though the horse pulled with all his might, the wagon still wouldn't move forward.

What's going on here, Zelig wondered.

Pronunciation Guide

despondent: di spon' dənt

from *D, My Name Is Danita*

by Norma Fox Mazer

"My poem is called, 'To Arnold With Whom I Used To Pick Raspberries When We Were Children Thirty-five Years Ago,'" I said.

"A bit louder, please." Mrs. Avora, sitting below the stage in the first row, tossed her purple scarf over her shoulder.

"My poem is called, 'To Arnold With Whom I Used To Pick Raspberries When We Were Children Thirty-five Years Ago,'" I repeated loudly.

"Is that the title, the whole thing?" Mrs. Avora asked.

"Yes." Why had I picked a poem with such a long title? My hands started sweating. "It's by a poet called Hilda Wilcox."

I looked at Laredo, who was sitting in the second row, to see how I was doing. I should have worn my glasses. Laredo's face was a blur. But I could see that she was jabbing a finger toward her mouth. We'd agreed on that signal if I wasn't speaking loudly enough.

"IT'S BY A POET CALLED HILDA WILCOX," I almost shouted.

"Danita, are you planning to repeat everything?" Mrs. Avora touched her hair. It was cut straight across her forehead. "I surely hope not."

"This poem is not what you usually think a poem is. It doesn't rhyme and it's not boring." I took a deep breath. Was I speaking clearly? I had a tendency to mumble in public. I had to remember to speak slowly and distinctly.

from *A Jar of Dreams*
by Yoshiko Uchida

37

Fiction

"I hate always being different and left out," I told Aunt Waka.

Aunt Waka was folding my kimono and *obi* on top of my bed, smoothing them out carefully so there would be no wrinkles. She wrapped them up again in the soft rice paper and tied them up just the way they were when she'd brought them. Then she put them aside and sat down on my bed.

"I think I understand how you feel, Rinko," she said in a soft whispery voice. "When I was young and couldn't run or play with my friends, they used to tease me and call me a cripple. They often made me cry."

I thought of the old photograph of Aunt Waka standing with the crutch. "But you were smiling anyway," I said, as if she'd know what I was remembering.

"Just because you're different from other people doesn't mean you're not as good or that you have to dislike yourself," she said.

She looked straight into my eyes, as if she could see all the things that were muddling around inside my brain.

"Rinko, don't ever be ashamed of who you are," she said. "Just be the best person you can. Believe in your own worth. And someday I know you'll be able to feel proud of yourself, even the part of you that's different . . . the part that's Japanese."

Pronunciation Guide

kimono: kə mō′ nō   *obi*: ō′ bē

38 Summer of the Locusts

Fiction

There was a haze in the Kansas air that hot August day in 1874. As Mary Nelson looked across the fields, the sun began to grow dim. "I think a dust storm's coming, Mother!" Mary shouted. As her mother stepped outside, the dark cloud drew nearer. A pattering sound began as dark bodies dropped from the cloud and struck the ground. Within minutes, Mary and her mother were caught in a hail of falling locusts—migrating grasshoppers.

On the ground, the swarm of locusts formed a living carpet, inches deep. As the swarm moved, it began to eat. Mary held her hands over her ears to shut out the sound of millions of insect jaws at work.

"The crops!" her mother cried. "They'll eat everything! Grab blankets. We can't save the corn, but if we cover the garden, we might be able to save some vegetables."

Over the next two days, the locusts ate. They ate the corn, the garden plants, grass, weeds, and the leaves and bark of trees. When all the plantlife was gone, they attacked wooden tool handles, fence rails, and even leather harnesses. When they had eaten everything that could be eaten, they flew off.

Mary and her mother looked at the bare soil. "We'll replant," her mother said. "We'll go on."

Pronunciation Guide

migrating: mī' grāt ing

The Kidnapping of John Paul Getty III

Italian police thought it was a hoax. They did not believe sixteen-year-old John Paul Getty III had been kidnapped. A ransom note had been sent to Getty's mother. But it did not convince them.

The note demanded $17 million for the boy's safe return.

Police had reasons to be dubious. Getty's grandfather was the richest man in the world. Yet young Paul was always running out of money. Just before he disappeared, he joked about his lack of funds. He knew a way to solve his money problems, he told friends with a laugh. All he had to do was stage his own "perfect kidnapping."

The weeks dragged by. Then, in November, something happened that changed everything. An envelope was sent to an Italian newspaper. When employees opened it, they found a gruesome sight. The envelope contained a note, a lock of Paul's red hair, and a human ear.

Medical experts checked out the ear. It *was* Paul's. The boy's father and grandfather were shocked. They now realized that the kidnapping was real. Fearing for Paul's life, they agreed to bargain with the kidnappers.

Five months after being kidnapped, John Paul Getty III was free. With Paul safe, the police turned their attention to catching the kidnappers. In late January 1974, police made their move. They arrested all eight kidnappers.

Pronunciation Guide

hoax: hōks
dubious: do͞o′ bē əs

gruesome: gro͞o′ səm

40

Nonfiction

from *Franklin D. Roosevelt*
by Sandra Woodcock

On October 24, 1929, prices on the New York Stock Exchange dropped rapidly. Five days later the stock market crashed. Many investors lost everything.

People lost confidence in the stock market. They would not put their money into business. Factories closed down, and people lost their jobs. Many companies went bankrupt.

The banks ran out of money for loans, so businesses could not recover. More people lost their jobs. Many people were now too poor to pay their rent or even to buy food.

At that time the government did not pay unemployment benefits to people out of work. Many people became homeless and had to beg for food. The country seemed to hit rock bottom.

However, [Franklin Delano] Roosevelt had some ideas about how to get the United States out of the mess. In 1932 Roosevelt asked the people of the United States to vote for him for president. He said they must get over their fear and have confidence again. He promised a new deal for the people.

Roosevelt went to as many states as he could. He made speeches every night. He was popular everywhere he went. The people liked him and trusted him. He smiled, he was confident, and he gave them hope.

Trouble in Montreal

Canadians knew there might be trouble. Still, on the night of March 17, 1955, hockey fans turned out in force. They packed the Forum in the Quebec city of Montreal. They were not in a happy mood. The most-hated man in Quebec had announced that he would be at the game. Sooner or later, a riot was sure to break out.

That most-hated man was Clarence Campbell, president of the National Hockey League. He had just suspended Maurice "The Rocket" Richard for the rest of the year. A week earlier, Richard had twice swung his hockey stick at another player. Such violent acts sometimes happen in hockey. Most of the time the players involved get a fine or a short suspension. But this time Campbell had cracked down really hard.

Richard was a superstar. He was the best player on the Montreal Canadiens. Without him, the team had little chance of winning the Stanley Cup.

Richard also was a symbol of great pride for the people of Quebec. Like most people from Quebec, Richard spoke French. That set him apart from people in other parts of Canada. Campbell was from an English-speaking part of Canada. So to some fans, it seemed as if Campbell was punishing not just a player or a team but every French speaker in Quebec.

Pronunciation Guide

Richard: ri shard'   Canadiens: cə nā' dē enz'

from *Martin Luther King, Jr.*

by Julia Holt

In the 1950s and before, segregation in Alabama and throughout the South was very strict. On the buses all the drivers were white. Black people had to sit at the back. One day in 1955 a black woman called Rosa Parks sat in a seat saved for white people. The driver told her to move but she did not. Rosa was arrested.

This made black people very angry. There was a boycott of the buses for a year until the bus company gave in, and black people could sit on any seat on the buses. Martin Luther King, Jr. was in charge of the boycott. Martin and Rosa Parks were the first black people to get on a bus after the boycott.

This made Martin famous, but he was also hated. He got 30 hate letters a day, and his house was bombed. Martin had beaten the bus company, but the violence still did not stop. Many black people were taken from buses and beaten up.

Now that Martin Luther King, Jr. was famous, people all over America wanted to hear him speak. He gave up his full-time job and worked part-time as a minister. This meant he could give his life to speaking and protesting for equal rights.

from "The Serial Garden"

by Joan Aiken

Mark ran across the fields to Miss Pride's shop at Sticks Corner and asked if she had any cornflakes.

"Oh, I don't think I have any left, dear," Miss Pride said woefully. "I'll have a look. . . . I think I sold the last packet a week ago Tuesday."

"What about the one in the window?"

"That's a dummy, dear."

Miss Pride's shop window was full of nasty, dingy old cardboard cartons with nothing inside them, and several empty display stands which had fallen down and never been propped up again. Inside the shop were a few small, tired-looking tins and jars, which had a worn and scratched appearance as if mice had tried them and given up. Miss Pride herself was small and wan, with yellowish gray hair; she rooted rather hopelessly in a pile of empty boxes. Mark's mother never bought any groceries from Miss Pride's if she could help it, since the day when she had found a label inside the foil wrapping of a cream cheese saying, "This cheese should be eaten before May 11, 1899."

"No cornflakes I'm afraid, dear."

"Any wheat crispies? Puffed corn? Rice nuts?"

"No, dear. Nothing left."

Pronunciation Guide

wan: wän

Skiing the Impossible

Is Kristen Ulmer out of her mind? You might think so when she describes some of the jumps she's made on skis. For instance, there was the time she flew through the air so out of control that she fainted from fear. Luckily, she didn't kill herself. Still, Ulmer didn't quit skiing. Instead, she went out looking for even bigger jumps.

Ulmer is one of a small band of extreme skiers who feel they have outgrown normal skiing. Normal ski trails are marked. Signs tell everyone how hard the different trails are. Green circles are easy paths for "snow bunnies." Blue squares are harder, but they can be skied by most good skiers. Black diamonds are steep trails for experts only. Black diamonds offer plenty of excitement for most people. But not for Kristen Ulmer and friends. They want to ski the impossible!

What qualifies as "impossible"? Some extreme skiers love to ski off cliffs. A man named Terry Cook does backflips off 60-foot cliffs. Some like to ski in the narrow openings between cliffs. Others enjoy the thrill of skiing down a glacier in Antarctica. Some choose to ski the summits of huge mountains in Asia. You get the point: extreme skiers live to prove that what seems impossible sometimes can be done.

from *Mahatma Gandhi*
by Mike Wilson

When Gandhi went back to India in 1915, he got a hero's welcome. People wanted him to fight for Home Rule, to get the British out of India.

But soon he settled on a little farm, to live the simple life of a Holy Man. He grew his own food and made his own cloth. People came for miles to hear his words of wisdom. His message to the British Raj was loud and clear: "It's time you left India." But to the people of India he still said: don't hit back at your enemy. "I want to change their minds, not kill them."

He called for all Indians to go on strike, but he called it a day of prayer and fasting, so it was a day of peaceful protest.

When there was fighting between Indians and British soldiers, Gandhi fasted. He ate no food for days and days, to remind people he hated violence. In the end people felt ashamed of their violence, and the fighting stopped. He said: "All through history, the way of Truth and Love has always won in the end."

India won independence in 1948. The British moved out, but fighting soon broke out between Hindus and Muslims.

Pronunciation Guide

Gandhi: gän' dē   Raj: räj

46

Portrait of a Lion

Inga and I were on assignment in Africa to write and photograph a magazine article on lions. After a long day of missed shots, we were tired and hot, and we began driving back to camp in our open car. Then Inga spotted a lioness in an acacia tree. It was asleep, stretched out on a limb perhaps 10 feet above the road.

"I'll snap her picture as we pass underneath," Inga said.

As we drove past, the lioness woke up and scowled down at us. "I missed the shot," said Inga. "Let's go around again." So we did, and then we tried a third time. By now the lioness was crouched, hindquarters high, front paws gathered under her chest. The black tuft on her heavy tail thumped on the bark. "She won't jump," Inga assured me as we approached a fourth time.

"Don't be so sure!" I snapped. Just as we reached the tree, the lioness snarled loudly. My foot jumped spasmodically off the gas pedal, and the car stalled. Now we were directly under the angry cat! I frantically tried to restart the engine, fully expecting the lioness to pounce. Inga kept taking pictures. The lioness's heavy scent was in my nose as the car came to life.

"These shots will be fantastic!" Inga cried as we sped away.

Pronunciation Guide

acacia: ə kā' shə   spasmodically: spaz mod' ik lē

from *Mary McLeod Bethune*

by Patricia and Fred McKissack

Growing up surrounded by a large and loving family gave Mary Jane a healthy attitude and a lot of self-confidence. One day, however, something happened that left her hurt and confused. She went to work with her mother. The girl who lived there asked Mary to play. They enjoyed each other's company, until Mary Jane picked up a book. She turned a few pages, wondering what the words meant.

"Put that book down," the girl said. "Come over here and I'll show you some pictures. Put the book down. You can't read!"

Mary Jane was shocked. For the first time, her confidence was shaken. But not for long. That night, she remembered the harsh words. It was true. She couldn't read. Even so, she let her fingers trace the words in the family Bible. "God willing, I'll read one day," she whispered.

A while later, a visitor came to the McLeod farm. Mary Jane stopped working to watch the beautiful stranger walking toward them. The woman introduced herself as Miss Emma Wilson, the new schoolteacher. She explained that the Presbyterian Mission Board had sent her to Mayesville to start a school for black children. Miss Wilson asked if Mr. McLeod would allow his children to attend.

Pronunciation Guide

Presbyterian: prez' bi tēr' ē ən

from *Little by Little*

by Jean Little

I liked [my teacher] Miss Marr a lot. And, even though we had only met an hour ago, I thought she liked me, too.

She was young and pretty and had a gentle voice. But that was not all. Like Mr. Johnston, she had had polio. As I listened to her passing out books behind me, I could hear her limping, first a quick step, then a slow one. The sound made me feel a little less lonely. My teacher would understand how it felt to be the only cross-eyed girl in Victory School.

"This is your desk, Jean," she had said.

It sat, all by itself, right up against the front blackboard. I was supposed to be able to see better there. I had not yet managed to make anyone understand that if I wanted to read what was written on the board, I would have to stand up so that my face was only inches away from the writing. Then I would have to walk back and forth, following the words not only with my eyes but with my entire body. If the writing were up at the top of the board, I would have to stand on tiptoe or even climb on a chair to be able to decipher it. If it were near the bottom, I would have to crouch down.

Pronunciation Guide

decipher: di sī' fər

49 Harvesting Rice

Fiction

It was harvest time in the Mekong Delta. At the beginning of the rainy season, the rice seedlings had been planted by hand. Trang and other young women had lined up ankle deep in the water of the flooded paddy field. Taking one seedling at a time, Trang had worked, stooped over, gently pushing each plant into the mud. Now the rice had ripened. Its golden stalks were ready to be cut.

Singing joyous harvest songs, Trang and her friends paddled their small boats quickly down the narrow canal to the paddy fields. The teenagers shouted happily as their boats almost collided, almost swamped—but never did.

Offerings of flowers, candles, and incense were made to the gods and goddesses who protect the earth and plants. Then the long, tiring work of harvest began. With a small sickle, Trang cut the rice stalks. She bound the stalks into sheaves and stacked them on a nearby boat. Other workers carried the sheaves to the threshing floor.

At noon, work stopped for a feast. Trang eagerly dipped her chopsticks into her bowl of rice, vegetables, and curried chicken. Then it was back to work. This would be a good harvest, with much rice to feed the people for the coming year.

Pronunciation Guide

Mekong Delta: mā' kong   del' tə   sheaves: shēvz

from *The Case of the Baker Street Irregular*

by Robert Newman

⚬⚬⚬

Dr. Watson ran his eye over the back page of the newspaper, folded it and dropped it to the floor.

"So you found the paper rather dull today," said Holmes.

"Yes, I did," said Watson. Then he turned. Holmes, sitting at his desk and going through one of his scrapbooks, had his back to him. "How did you know?"

"It usually takes you forty-three minutes to get through it. Today it only took you thirty-six." Holmes swung around. "If you're finished with it, may I have it?"

"Of course." Watson handed him the paper, watched as he opened it to an inside page, picked up his scissors and cut something out. "Did I miss something?"

"You may not have missed it, but apparently it didn't interest you. However it did interest me."

Watson got up and went over to the desk where Holmes was pasting the clipping into the scrapbook. It was captioned *Disturbance at the Empire Club.*

"Yes, I saw that. But when did you see it? You haven't read the paper yet."

"No. But you were holding it up when you ate your breakfast and it caught my eye."

"But why should it interest you?"

from *By the Highway Home*

by Mary Stolz

The night before the moving men were to come for their things, the house caught on fire.

The first Catty and Ginger knew about it was when their mother came into their room and said in a low urgent voice, "Girls, girls, wake up. You, too, Catty. No nonsense about it. We have to get out. Now."

Ginger was on her feet in a second, but Catty tried to burrow back toward sleep.

She felt her mother's hand shaking her roughly, heard her say, "Catty, I'm telling you to get up now, this minute!"

"What's going on?" Ginger asked. "What's that smell?"

"There's a fire in the basement, and your father thinks we should get out of the house. Now, put on some clothes but don't stop to pack anything or save anything, do you understand? And hurry!"

Catty's swirl of sleepiness disappeared like a fog patch. She was dressed as quickly as Ginger, and down the hall to Lexy's room, where the door stood open.

"Lexy," she called. "Lex, where are you?"

"He's here with us," her father shouted. There was an acrid smell now and the hall was beginning to fill with smoke, so that Catty could scarcely make out the figures of her family at the head of the stairs.

Pronunciation Guide

acrid: ak′ rid

from *Sitting Bull*

by Sheila Black

The Crow warrior on the other side could hardly believe his eyes. The Sioux coming toward him was only a boy, and he did not even have a real weapon. The Crow warrior raised his bow and fitted an arrow to it. But before he could fire—bam! [The boy called] Slow struck him on the arm with his coup stick, and the bow fell from the Crow's hand.

The other Sioux warriors quickly fell upon him, and within minutes the Crow lay dead.

When other Crows saw how quickly their fellow brave had been killed, they fled over the hills, leaving horses and provisions behind them.

The Sioux burst into a song. It had been a good day. But the greatest honor of the battle belonged to Slow, for it was he who had taken the first coup against the enemy.

The boy was brave.

In triumph, the war party made its way back to camp. Returns-Again rode at the head of the Sioux warriors with his son beside him. He was proud and wanted everyone to know what the boy had done.

In the family tepee, he painted the boy from head to toe with the black color of victory. Then, placing him on one of his finest horses, he led him slowly around the . . . camp while everyone looked on.

"My son is brave!" Returns-Again chanted.

Pronunciation Guide

Sioux: so͞o   coup: ko͞o

from *Breaking Through*

by Francisco Jiménez

What I feared most happened that same year. I was in my eighth-grade social studies class at El Camino Junior High School in Santa Maria. I was getting ready to recite the preamble to the Declaration of Independence, which our class had to memorize. I had worked hard at memorizing it and felt confident. While I waited for class to start, I sat at my desk and recited it silently one last time. . . . I was ready.

After the bell rang, Miss Ehlis, my English and social studies teacher, began to take roll. She was interrupted by a knock on the door. When she opened it, I saw the school principal and a man behind him. As soon as I saw the green uniform, I panicked. I felt like running, but my legs would not move. I trembled and could feel my heart pounding against my chest as though it too wanted to escape. My eyes blurred. Miss Ehlis and the officer walked up to me. "This is him," she said softly, placing her right hand on my shoulder.

"Are you Francisco Jiménez?" he asked firmly. His deep voice echoed in my ears.

"Yes," I responded, wiping my tears and looking down at his large, black shiny boots. At that point I wished I were someone else, someone with a different name.

Pronunciation Guide

preamble: prē′ am′ bəl

from *Deadly Ants*

by Seymour Simon

Suddenly a column of ants bursts forth. The ants lay down a scent trail as they move. Other ants begin to follow the trail the first ants have left.

The ants at the head of the column hardly seem to be brave leaders. They never move more than a few inches out in front. Even this forward march is caused by all the pushing going on behind them. After being pushed ahead, the leading ants quickly return to the sides of the column.

With the leading ants hanging back and the rear ants pushing ahead, the column finally forms a broad swarm. The swarm spreads out as it moves forward. A large raiding swarm may be sixty-five feet across and four to six feet deep.

The pressure of moving ants causes first one part of the swarm to break forward, then another. This results in a kind of encircling movement. In this way, small animals are caught and trapped by the wall of advancing ants. The ants grab any living thing which cannot manage to get away, and bring the soft pieces back to the nest.

The approach of a raiding swarm of army ants can be heard from quite a distance. There is a steady rattling and rustling of plants and leaves as the ants move along and small animals try to escape.

The Money Pit

In the summer of 1795, a teenaged Nova Scotia farm boy named Daniel McGinnis decided to do a little exploring. All his life he had heard stories about buried pirate treasure on Oak Island. In the middle of a clearing on the island, Daniel came across an ancient oak with a sawed-off limb. Directly underneath, the ground had sunk to form a saucer-shaped depression. Daniel could draw only one conclusion—pirate treasure was buried here.

The next day, Daniel rowed back to the island with two friends. Dreaming of gold coins, the three boys began digging. Two feet down they hit a layer of flagstones. At 10 feet they hit a layer of oak logs. Deeper and deeper they dug, finding two more layers of logs before they finally gave up, 30 feet down.

Since that long-ago time, more than a dozen teams of explorers have dug in that mysterious hole on Oak Island. In 1803 one team hit a wooden chest at 98 feet. When they returned to unearth it the next day, the shaft was flooded. Today the hole is more than 150 feet deep. Vast sums of money have been spent on what has come to be called the Money Pit. But the mystery of Oak Island remains a mystery.

from *Island of the Blue Dolphins*
by Scott O'Dell

I did not sleep much the night before I went to the place of the sea elephants. I thought again about the law that forbade women to make weapons. I wondered if my arrows would go straight and, if they did, would they pierce the animal's tough hide. What if one of the bulls turned on me? What if I were injured and then had to fight the wild dogs as I dragged myself homeward?

I thought about these things most of the night, but with the sun I was up and on my way to the place where the sea elephants lived.

When I reached the cliff, the animals had left the reef and gathered along the shore. Like gray boulders the bulls sat on the pebbly slope. Below them the cows and their babies played in the waves.

Perhaps it is not right to speak of young sea elephants as babies, for they are as large as a man. But they are still babies in many ways. They follow their mothers around, waddling along on their flippers like children learning to walk, making crying sounds and sounds of pleasure that only the young make.

Louis Braille's Magic Dots

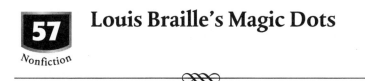

Louis Braille was born in 1809 and lived in a small town near Paris. As a baby, Louis could see perfectly. But an accident in his father's workshop left Louis blind at three years of age.

When he was old enough, Louis entered the town school. He wasn't expected to learn much, but Louis surprised people. He was soon at the top of his class, though he could not read or write.

At age ten, Louis received a scholarship and attended a school in Paris for blind boys. Reading was part of the school program. With their fingertips, students felt raised letters stamped on paper. They read slowly, letter by letter. It was difficult for students to tell the letters apart.

Soon another system of reading was introduced at the school. The system was based on a method that soldiers had used for reading messages in the dark. Readers would read groups of raised dots rather than letters. Different groups of dots stood for different sounds.

By age 15, Louis had developed a more efficient system. Fewer dots were used, and they were grouped to represent letters, not sounds. This helped students be sure of what they were reading.

When Louis became a teacher at the school he had attended, he taught his system to his students—a system he called Braille.

Pronunciation Guide

Braille: brāl

58

Fiction

from **"A Hanukkah Eve in Warsaw"**

by Isaac Bashevis Singer

Chunks of ice fell from the sky and a strong wind began to blow. Maybe the world was coming to an end? It seemed to me that there was thunder and lightning.

I started to run [home] and I fell several times. I picked myself up, and to my alarm I saw that I had strayed into some other street. Here, the streetlights weren't gas but electric. I saw a trolley that wasn't drawn by horses. The rod extending from its roof to the wires overhead sprayed bluish sparks. A fear came over me—I was lost! I stopped passersby and asked them directions, but they ignored me. One person did answer me, but in Polish, a language I had never learned. I could barely keep from crying. I wanted to turn back to where I had come from, but apparently I only strayed farther away. I passed brightly illuminated stores and a building with balconies and columns like some royal palace. Music was playing upstairs, and below, merchants were clearing away their goods from the stalls. The wind scattered kerchiefs, handkerchiefs, shirts, and blouses, and they whirled in the air like imps. That which I had always feared had apparently happened—the evil spirits had turned their wrath on me.

Now the wind thrust me forward.

Pronunciation Guide

illuminated: i loo′ mə nā′ tid

59 The 2,000-mile Ride

Nonfiction

In 1860 the Wild West was still wild. It stretched over mile after mile of wide grassy plains, dusty desert, and high mountains.

It took months to get from the East to California, and the trip was always dangerous. People died of sickness or from lack of water. Some were killed by American Indians, who were fighting to keep their land. The mail traveled very slowly across this land. By stagecoach, it could take two months for letters to reach California. Newspapers were always at least a month old by the time they reached the West coast.

Then some businessmen had a great idea. They would send the mail with messengers on fast horses. They would call this service the Pony Express.

One hundred ninety stations, ten to fifteen miles apart, were established from Missouri to California. Five hundred horses were purchased. Eighty riders were hired. Some were no more than boys. The average age of the riders was just eighteen.

Riders carried the mail in waterproof bags. When a rider arrived at a station, a fresh horse would be waiting. The rider would jump off his horse, grab the mailbags, and jump on the new horse. He was gone again in less than two minutes.

60

Fiction

from "Flight"

by John Steinbeck

⊶⊷⊶

Pepé started up, listening. His horse had whinnied. The moon was just slipping behind the western ridge, leaving the valley in darkness behind it. Pepé sat tensely gripping his rifle. From far up the trail he heard an answering whinny and the crash of shod hooves on the broken rock. He jumped to his feet, ran to his horse and led it under the trees. He threw on the saddle and cinched it tight for the steep trail, caught the unwilling head and forced the bit into the mouth. He felt the saddle to make sure the water bag and the sack of jerky were there. Then he mounted and turned up the hill.

It was velvet dark. The horse found the entrance to the trail where it left the flat, and started up, stumbling and slipping on the rocks. Pepé's hand rose up to his head. His hat was gone. He had left it under the oak tree.

The horse had struggled far up the trail when the first change of dawn came into the air, a steel grayness as light mixed thoroughly with dark. Gradually the sharp snaggled edge of the ridge stood out above them, rotten granite tortured and eaten by the winds of time.

Pronunciation Guide

whinnied: hwin' ēd   cinched: sinchd

Life Beneath the Snow

Nonfiction

Flake by flake, snow covers the ground. Fresh snow looks smooth and clean, but underneath, the ground is the same as it was in the fall. Fallen trees and leaves, rock piles and tall grass, are still there, but hidden from our view. The snow isn't a solid block. Under the snow are spaces and tunnels.

Many small animals live under the snow all winter long. One of the largest of these animals is the red squirrel. Most of the year, red squirrels live in trees, but when it gets cold, red squirrels build tunnels under the snow. There, they eat the pinecones they have stored.

Most of the year meadow voles live in underground burrows. When it is freezing cold and the ground begins to freeze, the meadow voles are in danger. Their burrows can't protect them from the weather.

Once it snows, life becomes easier for the meadow voles. The snow blanket keeps the ground warm, and the bottom layer of the snow becomes loose and easy to tunnel through. Meadow voles dig tunnels near their nests and eat all the plants they find. When the snow melts, you can tell where their tunnels were by noticing narrow trails of very short grass.

Pronunciation Guide

voles: vōlz

from **"Tennis"**

by Roger Angell

I play a game of tennis just like my father's. Oh, not as good. Not nearly as good, because I haven't had the experience. But it's the same game, really. I've had people tell me that when they saw us playing together—that we both made the same shot the same way. Maybe my backhand was a little better (when it was on), and I used to think that my old man didn't get down low enough on a soft return to his forehand. But mostly we played the same game. Which isn't surprising, seeing that he taught me the game. He started way back when I was about nine or ten. He used to spend whole mornings with me, teaching me a single shot. I guess it was good for me and he did teach me a good, all-around game, but even now I can remember that those morning lessons would somehow discourage both of us. I couldn't seem to learn fast enough to suit him, and he'd get upset and shout across at me, "Straight arm! Straight arm!", and then *I'd* get jumpy and do the shot even worse. We'd both be glad when the lesson ended.

Hidden in the Dark

One afternoon four young men—armed with a knife, a small oil lamp, and a rope—made an amazing discovery. Earlier, one of the boys had noticed a deep hole in the ground next to a newly fallen tree. He asked his friends if they wanted to go exploring with him. He said they might find buried treasure. The year was 1940, and the place was southern France.

When the boys reached the hole, they cleared stones away from its entrance. Then they lowered themselves into the dark. They found that the hole was a passageway into a large cave. When they played the dim light of their lamp on the cave walls, they were amazed to see colorful paintings. The paintings showed red cows, yellow horses, and black bulls and stags racing across the walls and ceiling of the cave. The young men had indeed found a treasure, even though it was not the kind they had expected.

Excited by their discovery, they returned the next day. They searched farther into what turned out to be a series of caves. All around them were mysterious paintings. The boys couldn't keep this news to themselves. They told their families and friends. When the villagers heard about the paintings, they hurried to see the site. Soon the scientists followed.

from *Dragon's Gate*

by Laurence Yep

Getting out the fuse, I got everything ready and then reached for the matches. Whether because of the wind or my own nervousness, the first one wouldn't light. Neither would the second.

Until now, I had never thought of asking my father or mother for anything. Help me, I begged silently as I tried to strike the next match. Gratefully I watched it flare into life; and I used my free hand to protect the fragile flame until it rose tall and strong.

Carefully I lowered it to the fuse. The fire caught and sputtered. My first impulse was to run, but I cupped my hands around the fuse tip until I was sure it would go on burning. Then I turned and began to high-step back along my tracks. I was among the ice flowers halfway down the cliff when the rock shook and I heard a loud roar. The snow above me heaved, and bushels of it spilled down around me.

Suddenly the noise of the explosion was drowned out by an even louder sound—a huge roar as if from a giant throat—as if the [mountain] itself was full of a great rage. I had done it. I had started the avalanche.

Pronunciation Guide

fragile: fraj′ əl   avalanche: av′ ə lanch′

from *How Green Was My Valley*

by Richard Llewellyn

And then I found him.

Up against the coal face, he was, in a clearance that the stone had not quite filled.

I put my candle on a rock, and crawled to him, and he saw me, and smiled.

He was lying down, with his head on a pillow of rock, on a bed of rock, with sheets and bedclothes of rock to cover him to the neck, and I saw that if I moved only one bit, the roof would fall in.

He saw it, too, and his head shook, gently, and his eyes closed.

He knew there were others in the tunnel.

I crawled beside him, and pulled away the stone from under his head, and rested him in my lap.

"Willie," I said, "tell them to send props, quick."

I heard them passing the message down, and Willie trying to pull away enough rock to come in beside me.

"Mind, Willie," I said, "the roof will fall."

"Have you found him?" Willie asked me, . . . scraping through the dust.

"Yes," I said, and [had] no heart to say more.

My father moved his head, and I looked down at him, sideways to me, and tried to think what I could do.

from *The River*

by Gary Paulsen

⟋⟍⟍⟋⟍⟋

The rain came about eleven.

Derek had time for one quick joke.

"You said it would be six and a half hours—it's almost seven."

Then it hit them and there was nothing but water. The clouds had come quickly, covering the stars and moon in what seemed like minutes and then just opened up and dropped everything on them.

It wasn't just a rain. It was a roaring, ripping downpour of water that almost drove them into the ground.

They had moved back into the lean-to to try to get some rest since the mosquitoes partially lessened, but the temporary roof did nothing, absolutely nothing, to slow the water.

They were immediately soaked, then more soaked, sloppy with water.

They tried moving beneath some overhanging thick willows and birch near the edge of the lake, but the trees also did nothing to slow the downpour and finally they just sat, huddled beneath the willows, and took it.

I have, Brian thought, always been wet.

Always.

Even my soul is wet.

He felt the water running down his back. He judged it to be about the same rate as the faucet in his kitchen sink at home.

The Pride of Paris

As it was being built more than a hundred years ago,
some thought the strange tower would collapse. Others
said it was ugly. It ruined the beautiful Paris skyline.
Now people come from all over the world to see it—the
Eiffel Tower.

In 1889 the French government was to host the
world's fair in Paris. The fair was especially important
to the French government. It gave France the chance to
impress the world with the greatness of Paris and of their
country. Now people would see how much had changed
in France in the one hundred years since the French
Revolution! The government commissioned a grand
structure to be built. Gustave Eiffel was appointed to
build what would be the tallest structure in the world,
a structure that would bear his name.

Work on the tower began in 1887. Nothing like it
had ever been built before. Some builders were not happy
with the plans. A professor said that the tower should
not be higher than 700 feet tall. Some artists and writers
claimed that the tower looked like a big black chimney.
They said its crude looks and large size ruined the views
of Paris's churches and museums.

But work continued. And by March 1889—in time
for the fair—the whole tower was finished.

Pronunciation Guide

Gustave Eiffel: gəs tav′   ī′ fəl

from *A Long Way from Chicago*
by Richard Peck

Grandma was rowing out from the bank. Now she was putting up the oars and standing in the boat. It rocked dangerously, though she planted her big boots as wide as the sides allowed. She reached down for the long rod with the hook at the end.

Glancing briefly into the brown water, she plunged the rod into the creek. It hit something, and she began to pull the rod back up, hand over hand. She was weaving to keep her balance in the tipping boat. I wanted to hang on to the sides, but pictured a cottonmouth rearing up and sinking fangs in my hand.

Something broke the surface of the creek, something on a chain Grandma had hooked. It was bigger than the picnic hamper and looked like an orange crate, streaming water. And inside: whipping tails and general writhing.

I thought of cottonmouths and ducked. But they were catfish, mad as hornets, who'd been drawn by Grandma's terrible cheese [bait]. She heaved in the crate and unlatched the top. In the bottom of the boat was a wire-and-net contraption that expanded as she filled it with wiggling fish. . . . Grandma kept at it, bent double in the boat. She was as busy as a bird dog, one of her own favorite sayings.

Pronunciation Guide

writhing: rīth′ ing

He stepped through the doors and walked across the sidewalk. The air outside was hot and muggy, like an oven after the walk through the air-conditioned terminal. The late-afternoon sun put a bright glare on everything. Ted blinked in the sunlight and walked toward a cabbie leaning on the front fender of his cab.

"Comiskey Park?" he asked.

"Yes, sir." The cabbie came off the fender, walked around the front of the cab, and got in behind the wheel.

Ted opened the back door and tossed his canvas bag, with the bat attached, into the backseat and climbed in behind it.

"You a ball player?" the driver asked as he wheeled the taxi past the rows of terminals and around the O'Hare Hilton Hotel and the huge parking deck, heading for the Kennedy Expressway into the city.

"Yep."

"White Sox?"

"Nope. I'm the new third baseman for the Royals," Ted said. Then he added "The Kansas City Royals."

"New third baseman, huh? What's your name?"

"Ted Bell."

"Ted Bell," the driver repeated. He leaned forward and to his right, glancing at Ted in his rearview mirror. "What's happening to Lou Mills?"

Ted had heard the question before.

from *The Edge of Next Year*

by Mary Stolz

Orin was aware at first only of sounds. The shattering of glass, the earsplitting crash of metal against the tree trunk. Even when all he could hear was the drumming of rain on the roof, he sat with his eyes closed, afraid of what he'd see if he opened them, afraid to try his voice. His body trembled violently, and the sound of rain on the roof was like an assault. He heard, then, the screech of tires on the wet road as people slowed, or braked to a stop. He heard voices, shouts. He heard screams. But he sat with his eyes closed, not daring to put a hand out to see if [his brother] Victor was there beside him, was all right, was alive. He sat in his own darkness, surrounded now by yelling and motion in the world outside the car, but he was alone and terrified and willfully blind.

He started with a cry when a hand gripped his arm.

"Come on, son," said a strange voice. "Come along. We'll put you over there in the cruiser, and you can wait there. It's warm in the cruiser, you'll be better there."

Orin leaned away from the hand, pressing his shoulder blades against the seat. "Lemme alone," he said softly. "Please. I want to—"

"Son, you'll have to get out of this car."

Stone Age Weapons

Fiction

The Neanderthal toolmaker chose a stone. One of a long line of toolmakers, he knew which stones were best. This stone was especially desirable—it was flint. By striking the stone in the correct way, he could make it break as he chose.

Tribe members watched in awe as the toolmaker struck the flint with his striking stone to expose its solid central core. He examined the piece of flint closely and decided it would make a good hand ax.

The toolmaker struck the flint with his hammer. With each blow, large, sharp chips fell away until the flint had the rough shape of a hand ax. Now he chose another tool, a bone hammer, to shape the edges of the ax. Smaller pieces fell away, making the edges of the ax thin and sharp.

The toolmaker examined the new ax. About five inches long, with sharp edges on either side, it could be used to chop wood, kill a large animal, or butcher meat. The chips that had fallen from its sides would make smaller weapons—knives and spearheads. In an age when tools and weapons were the same, these were the basic tools of Neanderthal existence.

Pronunciation Guide

Neanderthal: nē an′ dər thôl′

From a Family of Musicians:
Wynton Marsalis

⌘

Wynton Marsalis was born in 1961, in a town just outside of New Orleans. Wynton's family was musical. His father was a jazz pianist and a music teacher. His brother played the piano and the saxophone. Music surrounded him, and at twelve, Wynton became a musician too. He took up the trumpet, and he never put it down again.

Wynton works hard at anything he does. That was his approach to learning to play the trumpet, too. He practiced—morning, noon, and night. As a teen, he was an excellent student. And he continued to practice. Sometimes even after everyone in his house had gone to bed, Wynton went outside. He practiced under the stars.

Wynton's perseverance and hard work were rewarded. His talent and ability were hard to ignore. When he was eighteen, he attended a famous music school in New York City. At school, he studied classical music. Most classical music is from Europe, and much of it is quite old. Wynton knew that a complete musician should know all kinds of music. He liked playing the classics. But he was beginning to understand that his heart belonged to another type of music. His heart belonged to jazz.

Pronunciation Guide

Wynton Marsalis: win' tən   mär sal' əs

Acknowledgments

Grateful acknowledgment is given to the authors and publishers listed below for brief passages excerpted from these longer works.

from *Watership Down* by Richard Adams. Copyright © 1972 by Rex Collings Ltd. Macmillan Publishing Company.

from "Tuesday of the Other June" by Norma Fox Mazer. In *Short Takes: A Short Story Collection for Young Readers,* ed. Elizabeth Segel. Copyright © 1986 by Elizabeth Segel. Dell Publishing, a division of Bantam Doubleday Dell Publishing Group.

from *Homesick: My Own Story* by Jean Fritz. Copyright © 1982 by Jean Fritz. Penguin Putnam.

from *Benjamin Franklin: Printer, Inventor, Statesman* by David A. Adler. Copyright © 1992 by David A. Adler. Holiday House.

from *The Curse of the Blue Figurine* by John Bellairs. Copyright © 1983 by John Bellairs. Bantam Skylark.

from *The Exxon Valdez: Tragic Oil Spill* by Victoria Sherrow. Copyright © 1998 by Enslow Publishers.

from *Dragonwings* by Laurence Yep. Copyright © 1975 by Laurence Yep. HarperCollins Publishers.

from *Charlotte Forten: Free Black Teacher* by Esther M. Douty. Copyright © 1971 by Esther M. Douty. Garrard Publishing Company.

from *The Moon of the Moles* by Jean Craighead George. Copyright © 1969 by Jean Craighead George. Thomas Y. Crowell Company.

from *Within Reach: My Everest Story* by Mark Pfetzer and Jack Galvin. Copyright © 1998 by Mark Pfetzer and Jack Galvin. Puffin Books.

from *The Pistachio Prescription* by Paula Danziger. Copyright © 1978 by Paula Danziger. Bantam Doubleday Dell Books for Young Readers.

from *Dark Harvest: Migrant Farmworkers in America* by Brent Ashabranner. Copyright © 1985 by Brent Ashabranner. Dodd, Mead & Company.

from *I Have Lived a Thousand Years* by Livia Bitton-Jackson. Copyright © 1997 by Livia E. Bitton-Jackson. Simon & Schuster Books for Young Readers.

from *The Black Stallion* by Walter Farley. Copyright © 1941 and renewed 1968 by Walter Farley. Random House.

from "Stop the Sun" by Gary Paulsen from *Boy's Life,* January 1986. Copyright © 1986 by Gary Paulsen.

from *So Big* by Edna Ferber. Copyright © 1924 and renewed 1952 by Edna Ferber. University of Illinois Press.

from *Taking Sides* by Gary Soto. Copyright © 1991 by Gary Soto. Harcourt Brace & Company.

from "Snowfall in Childhood" from *Actor's Blood* by Ben Hecht. Copyright © 1936 by Ben Hecht. Covici Friede Publishers.

from *The Autobiography of Miss Jane Pittman* by Ernest J. Gaines. Copyright © 1971 by Ernest J. Gaines. Bantam Books.

from *Think Like an Eagle: At Work with a Wildlife Photographer* by Kathryn Lasky. Copyright © 1992 by Kathryn Lasky. Little, Brown and Company.

from *Laura: The Life of Laura Ingalls Wilder* by Donald Zochert. Copyright © 1976 by Donald Zochert. Avon Books.

from *The Contender* by Robert Lipsyte. Copyright © 1967 by Robert M. Lipsyte. Bantam Books.

from *Lost Star: The Story of Amelia Earhart* by Patricia Lauber. Copyright © 1988 by Patricia G. Lauber. Scholastic.